PAGES FROM A WIDOW'S TEARS

A Memoir

JULIET CLARKE

PAGES FROM A WIDOW'S TEARS

A Memoir

JULIET CLARKE

Copyright © 2022 Juliet Clarke

All rights reserved. No part of this book may be used
or reproduced by any means, graphic, electronic, or mechanical,
including photocopying, recording, taping, or by any information
storage retrieval system without the written permission
of the author except in the case of brief quotations
embodied in critical articles and reviews.

All rights reserved.

ISBN# 978-1-5136-9868-7

Library of Congress Control Number: 2022917766

PO Box 4455 | Wilmington NC
www.nuvisiondesigns.biz

Printed in the United States of America.

TABLE OF CONTENTS

My Village 7

Dedication 9

Acknowledgements 11

Introduction 13

Chapter 1: And So, It Began 19

Chapter 2: Life As Mrs. Joaquin Chinyelu Clarke 27

Chapter 3: "My Momma, What's Up Jazz, Hi Dad" 39

Chapter 4: I Got To The Gold 47

Chapter 5: The Worst Night Of My Life 53

Chapter 6: Celebrating The Life Of My Yummy 69

Chapter 7: Dark 83

Chapter 8: Light 91

Chapter 9: What I Learned 99

MY VILLAGE

There is absolutely no way I could have made it through this process without the amazing village of people God placed in my life. It's one thing for people to say that they love you. It's totally different to experience that love in a tangible way when you're at your lowest point in life. My village played a pivotal role in bringing me back to life either publicly or privately, and I will be forever grateful to you. I love you all!!

Juliet

DEDICATION

This book is dedicated to the memory of my husband, Joaquin Chinyelu Clarke, RN BSN. It was my absolute joy to be your wife. You enriched my life in ways that cannot be expressed in words. While your physical absence was not the healing of my desire, my enduring love for you helped me to accept your request and GOD's sovereign will. You are now free and that means more to me than you will ever know. I will forever love you.

Mrs. Joaquin Clarke

ACKNOWLEDGEMENTS

My immediate family has always been my strongest support system. Thank you, Mommy, Daddy, and Jasmine, for praying me through and at times carrying me through this most difficult time.

To Dr. Phyllis Carter who has always been an integral part of my life, thank you for your wise words of counsel and for calling strength out of me that I did not know was there.

To Dr. Wanda Davis who gave me the guidance to better understand how to not give up on God or myself in the midst of the worst storm I have ever experienced.

To Pastor Cordelia Wallace for her private impartation that helped me to reframe my perspective of God during my darkest hour.

To Elder Dora Smith who gave insight from her known experience of losing a spouse. Every message was so appreciated. Thank you for showing me how to use ***the widow's might*** (your ministry) to get through the darkness.

Last but not least, to Apostle Wynell Freeman who has always been there to snatch me back to reality when I was at my lowest points, and I considered possibly making disastrous decisions when listening to what the enemy had tried to convince me to do. Thank you for standing in the gap when I was too weak to fight for myself.

INTRODUCTION

"Mrs. Clarke, according to the monitor your husband has passed on."

— ·· — ·· — ·· — ·· — ·· — ·· — ·· — ·>

The instant those words hit the air I couldn't breathe. My friend Tera, who had been with me along with my father, took my hand, and we walked out of that hospital room and off the ICU unit for the last time. I honestly can't recall the specific details of what happened next. It was all a blur.

Fifty-nine days before our third wedding anniversary, MY HUSBAND DIED.

My Father's close friend, the late Dr. Arthur Holmes had a saying, *"There is nothing more final than death."* As with many things in life, I didn't fully comprehend the depth of that statement until I experienced it myself. Until this point, the closest experiences with death I had was the passing of my maternal grandmother, and then my spiritual grandmother. Both were devastating, but this was different. Now that I had to check the box that said "widow", I experienced it in a way that had become emotionally tangible.

I tend not to take the position of an "authority" on any subject as I am keenly aware of all the things that I don't know. One never knows nearly as much as they believe they do. There's always room to learn more. However, I will take the liberty to share from a place of first-hand experience on the subject. For me, the death of my husband was the most disorienting thing I have ever experienced in my personal life. Until then, for the most part, I'd lived a predictable life. I like the familiar, I enjoy routine and I find comfort in it. As the saying goes, opposites attract, and my husband thrived on change and new experiences. This made for such interesting exchanges within marriage: mostly comical, some combustible, but never boring. I like knowing what I'll be doing five weeks from now at 3:15 pm. Having a plan, a backup plan, and a plan in case that plan doesn't work, gives me comfort. My plan was for us to stay married for many years, have children, and age together. My husband, going home to be with the Lord two- and one-half years after our wedding, was definitely, not on my schedule. To stand before almost three hundred of our closest friends and family members and commit ourselves to one another, only to have many of those same people return to watch me say goodbye to him, was a trauma that in many ways I am still processing. What word describes an atomic bomb exploding right in front of your face? Instantly, I went from being a sure and trusting person to becoming untrusting, unsure, and afraid of everything. I couldn't depend on anything: not my thoughts, not myself, and for the sake of being honest, not even God. Yup. ***I admit I lost all my faith and trust in God.*** Okay. So, before we continue, let me just lay some ground rules for your reading pleasure. *Please understand that I have every intention of being completely honest and fully transparent.* While I know transparency is sometimes frowned upon, for the sake of my freedom, I promise that I will graciously tell you the truth of my experience. So yes, this bible-believing, tongue-talking, raised in church all my life, bishop's daughter, ordained elder lost all my faith, hope, and trust in God. All the lights went out in my life, and the darkness became an unfamiliar constant. Remember, routine is comforting to me and at this time in my life, nothing resembled anything like what I had grown accustomed to it being.

> This book is about my journey from the bondage of that darkness to the freedom of light. Please understand that I am not in any way shape or form an "expert" about grief. I write first, to free myself and then, to help you, if you find yourself in any form of darkness, be it grief or any other reason, please know that THERE IS HOPE! I know that for sure. So, that's why I'm confident to share that with you.

My journey was ugly, violent and at times humiliating. Being that it is in fact a journey, it is all those things as well as funny, hopeful and yes, I can now even say beautiful. So, grab a cup of coffee, or tea, or your favorite glass of wine (saints don't judge the journey, it's different for everybody…lol!) and hopefully find some inspiration and encouragement in the next few pages of this hot crispy mess of a journey I found myself on. I pray it helps!

CHAPTER 1
AND SO, IT BEGAN

I am aware that there's a bit of curiosity surrounding where my husband and I met and how it all came to be. Being a "PK" (Preacher's Kid), growing up in church, I was earmarked to be a "preacher's wife." That's just the way it goes in my world. It's not bad. It's not good. It's just what it is. There was only one problem. I wanted absolutely no parts of it. I saw how ministry takes a toll on a marriage, and a first family and I didn't want to continue to live my life on the front row. I had decided long before I met my husband that I did not want to share him. I wanted him all to myself. I see how that can sound selfish, but to give perspective, growing up I had to share my parents, my life, my energy, and everything else and I wanted my husband for myself. Someone that would be all mine. Remember, I promised you complete honesty.

My church was founded by my parents when I was one years old, in the living room of our home. So, it's not an exaggeration to say that "The Fountain" (Fountain of Life Church Inc.) is like my sibling. There are people who have been a part of the church since the very beginning. Some of them knew my mom and dad prior to the inception of the church. Some of them watched my mother carry me. Let me say that as the "PK" experience goes, mine has been generally good. Some things just go along with being part of a first family. In the "Black Church" the first family still has a bit of mystique surrounding it. My parents taught my sister and I that being in the first family meant that we were called to serve. My parents primarily, my sister and I secondarily. We served them in any way shape or form. Me being the firstborn, I took this instruction to heart, and to this day there isn't anything I haven't done or wouldn't do to serve my church or the people in it. Honestly, I found joy in serving, and I still do. The people in my church are amazing. They love my parents and my sister and I, and they are very easy to serve. Many of them are an extension of my family.

As I began to go through the normal coming-of-age situations, I found it to be challenging from time to time.

Interacting with peers within the church presented some difficulties. I always found myself fighting the preconceived notion that I was "bratty" and "stuck up". I never thought of myself as better than anyone just because my father was their pastor, but for some reason that was the narrative surrounding me. This began a pattern of "people pleasing" as an attempt to "prove" that I wasn't that way. Exhausting work to say the least.

By the grace of God, my parents were able to provide my sister and I with a blessed life. This created some uncomfortable confrontations with my peer group. My parents had a healthy expectation that I would fulfill certain responsibilities within the ministry. That is the plight of the "PK". Our parents are called into ministry, we are born into it. So, sing, preach, play, administrate, pick one, two, or three, but you better do something. It's not bad or good. Just the way it is. My mother was a formidable presence within the ministry, particularly during the early years. My father prayed, preached, prophesied, and casted the vision. I watched my mother support him in every aspect of his expression of his calling.

Juliet Clarke

You didn't see my dad without seeing my mom. The ministry grew from our living room and my mom was right there for every step of the journey. I always wanted to be just like my mom. In my eyes, there is nothing she can't do. At one point in her life, she was a caregiver to both her parents, a pastor's wife, a travel agent, a counselor, and a mom. She managed to keep all those balls in the air, and nothing missed a beat. She wore the most beautiful jewelry (much of which I borrow often with protest). So, to say the least, it came as a shock when due to health challenges my mom was no longer able to physically attend church. Around the same time, her assistant got married and relocated which indirectly left it all to me. What a transition; from working as secondary support to becoming a part of the engine that ran the ministry. I was terrified and insecure in my ability to be able to do it. With the grace of God, he helped me to adjust to my new level of responsibilities. At the same time ministry began to call my dad out on the road which meant I had to support him at home in the pulpit. As support to my dad and as an ordained elder, I assumed the role of preaching in my father's absence. I became consumed with assuming these roles, on one side the natural, the other side the spiritual, and somewhere in the middle was my confusion, frustration, exhaustion, and frankly quiet resentment at this unexpected turn that my life had taken. From the time I was a child, I wanted to be three things: a teacher, a wife, and a mommy. Being a church administrator and preacher was not part of my life's plan.

Then there was the element of the people. Generally speaking, my mother's physical absence was handled well. However, as with anything in life, human nature is human nature, and the church is no different. I don't think I have to go into detail about how boundary lines can get blurry for some when the first lady is not physically present consistently. Like any PK I was ever ready to assist anyone in clarifying any blurriness that may have occurred so that those boundary lines remained in place and respected. For all these reasons and more, I had made an inner vow to myself that I would not under any circumstance marry a preacher. When I would say that many would laugh and say that I was in denial. Others told me that that wasn't

God's will for my life. Funny how people can assume the role of an expert on what GOD's will for your life is, but I digress. All I knew was that I didn't want to share. Being married to a pastor, being a PK inadvertently means you must share. You always have to be on, whether you want to be or not. I wanted to go somewhere and sit down and focus on being a teacher, a wife, and a mommy. One thing about confessions or saying something repeatedly is that it will manifest, so, be very careful what you say because what you say is what you will get.

    Joaquin Chinyelu Clarke walked into my life, and I was never the same. We met through a mutual friend. He inquired about me from our mutual friend and then searched for me on social media. He said that he "followed me" for a while to make sure I wasn't crazy. You'll come to learn from me that my husband was not one to bite his tongue. He was funny: really, really, funny. He was also a deep thinker and not intimidated by the dynamics of my personality. He could keep up with me. He loved music, he loved sports, he loved God, and he loved me. I always say I fell in love with him in his car.

No, not because of that! Because it was nothing for him to call me up and say, "I'll be there in 15 minutes, be ready to go." He would pull up; I would get in and off we would go to some adventure which included a great experience and usually an amazing plate of food.

Remember, I am a creature of habit. I even eat the same thing at the same few restaurants I frequent. I marveled at how he always tried something different, and he always found a new experience. I have lived in the same region my whole life and it would amaze me that he would find new beaches, new restaurants, and new things that I never experienced before him. He could talk to me, but most of all he could listen to me. He understood that while I was strong externally and internally, I was quite tender and had to be handled with care. From day one, I felt safe with him and that never changed. He was all mine. I didn't have to share him. **AND HE WASN'T A PREACHER.** He was a registered nurse administrator, and he loved his job, and may I say, he was very good at it.

Our relationship developed consistently and after a few months of talking, I kind of knew what direction we were headed in. After our first date, he told me he had to meet my dad because there was an age difference between us, him being almost 10 years my senior. I was so nervous about that meeting, because I really liked him, and I knew the like was on the verge of turning into love very quickly. Joaquin and my father met, and we continued to date until Christmas of 2017 when he asked me to marry him. I said, "Yes," and it was off to the races of wedding planning. Oh, what an experience that was. I must say my parents gave me a beautiful wedding. Not to sound so cliché but it really was a fairytale. My mother was the CEO of my wedding, and my dad was the financier. ***It really was a dream.***

CHAPTER 2
LIFE AS MRS. JOAQUIN CHINYELU CLARKE

My husband could make me laugh from the inside out. That was just one of the many things I loved about him. I tend to color inside the lines, follow the rules, check the boxes, and get home before the street lights come on. Joaquin was the exact opposite. He colored wherever he could find clear space on paper. One of the joys of his life was traveling with a gospel choir internationally. As he would tell it, as soon as he got off the plane he'd check into the hotel, rent a bike, grab a local map, and explore whatever country he happened to be in, with his camera close at hand. I wish I could share with you the countless pictures he took. True to his adventurous nature, these photos ranged from the bottom of a dormant volcano in the Azores to the mountain tops of Scotland. He was an adventurer at heart. He made enjoying life his hobby. He helped me to understand intrinsically by example that life is meant to be lived. His personality was large, and his laughter was infectious. I can still hear it in my head. The number of times I couldn't hold my sides together in laughter can't be counted. His eyes were captivating, one of my favorite things to do was get lost in them. He could see me. Really see me. My feelings, my thoughts, my emotional needs. I can get stuck in my head more than I would like to admit and he was very good at opening the door and showing me the way out.

Joaquin loved music, great food, and traveling but his ultimate love (I'm not ashamed to admit even over and above me) was the New York Football Giants. The thing I loved most about watching him be a fan was no matter how bad they played he still stayed loyal to them. No matter the score, the play, or the fumble, he was always right there front and center, wearing his Giants jersey and hat (the way he always watched a home game) screaming to the top of his lungs.

Joaquin was an "all-in" type of person. He didn't do anything in a haphazard way, and he always liked to know everything there was to know about a subject matter (and he usually did). His certainty and confidence were such a turn-on to me. Nothing intimidated him. If he didn't know it, he would find out about it and then come back and tell you three things you didn't know about whatever it was he had just learned about.

One of the things that I loved about my husband was that he was unpredictable. Likewise, it's also one of the things that drove me completely crazy about him also. We never ate at the same restaurant twice. He never even rode home from church the same way. I was in the lines. He was out of the lines. I was black and white, and he lived in the gray. What I didn't realize was that he was exactly what I needed at that time. Joaquin taught me how important it is to live life rather than just accomplish goals and get through.

Now here is where things begin to get a bit sticky. The other side of my husband's personality could sometimes turn people off. In fact, there were a few voices that expressed concern over his way of unbiasedly sharing what he felt. I want to univocally say that I absolutely loved my husband. However, I am very clear about who he was. My Nana would always tell me; you can love a man but you have to be clear about how he is even if that's an understanding you keep to yourself. He was unapologetically him. There were times when I wished that he would use a filter. There were times when I wished that he just kept his thoughts to himself rather than sharing everything that popped into his head. The fact is that like every wife, even though that was an aspect of my husband that I wished he would change, he didn't. My husband had a personality that was larger than some people could accommodate. He was the type of person that could not be in a space and that space does not know he was there. Unapologetically bold, my husband was the type to let his thoughts be common knowledge.

Having a voice that is heard and valued is so important to the growth and development of a child. For any reason, if that voice is attacked, diminished, or silenced that child will grow up to become an adult who values their own voice over sensibility just for the sake of being heard. An explanation is not an excuse; it just comes to serve as material to help understand the presentation of certain things. My husband would tell it straight from his mind: no sugar, no salt, just raw and uncut. Anyone who followed him on social media saw that he clearly didn't mind being controversial.

Older, wiser women would often counsel and encourage me to simply let him be. They would encourage me to pray about the things that caused me challenges. As our time together progressed, I saw how God was able to heal that aspect of his personality to the extent that he would allow it. The truth is I saw the wisdom in the counsel of the women who encouraged me to leave him to God because I needed that aspect of his personality when I was unable to speak up for myself. Now if you are reading this and you happen to know me personally, I'm sure your eyebrows may have furloughed a bit at the thought of me needing anyone to "speak up" for me. Hence, it is true. As outspoken as I may present, there were times when my presentation and my inner reality did not match. I didn't always do a good job of advocating for myself.

One of the ways that the Lord used Joaquin was as a model for me of what balance looked like. Coming from a ministry family, church work was just what we did. The nature of church work is to be all-consuming and take you away with it. There's always something that needs to be done and someone who needs a bit of extra tender loving care. When my husband came into my life I was consumed with "doing" and he helped me to learn how to enjoy "being."

I believe that one of the ways we as human beings attempt to heal ourselves is by providing what we may need emotionally but didn't receive. Joaquin had the innate ability to see people, particularly people that were hurting. One memory I will always hold dear to my heart is watching him pray for a man in distress at a local cemetery. I had been filling in for my dad at a graveside service and Joaquin drove me. As we were leaving, he saw a man sitting on a bench with an open bottle of Jack Daniels. I'm not ashamed to admit I kept looking at the time as I had to get back to the church by a certain time to help serve at the repast. Joaquin, not moved by my anxious energy, stopped and asked the man if he was okay. When the man acknowledged that this day was the first anniversary of his father's passing and he wasn't doing a good job handling it, Joaquin began to talk to him. He asked him questions about his father and told him stories of how he coped with his own father's passing. After talking with the man for a moment, he asked him if he could pray with him. When the man agreed, I watched my husband pray for this man with such intensity that it made me feel a little convicted. Here I was wearing the clergy collar and I didn't even see the man, while he not only saw him but discerned his need and created a space where God could touch him. *That was the side of my husband that I loved so much. His ability to see people and validate their existence.*

I was blessed to spend six of my husband's forty-nine birthdays with him: three of them as his wife.

I made sure that his birthdays were special events in our lives. One year I decided to turn our spare bedroom into a Giants man cave for him. My goal was to give him a space that was all his own. This being more an act of marital survival than anything else. I had grown tired of seeing cups on my glass-top coffee tables in the living room. My Aunt Vanessa came over and we went to work. When we were done a few minutes before he was due to be back home, I asked a few of his friends and our family to come over and help celebrate his birthday. When he opened the door for the first time, he stood speechless in the doorway. Knowing Joaquin, speechless was not an adjective that could commonly describe him. I made him a three-layer Giants cake and true to his nature, he made sure everyone realized that it slightly leaned to one side. Three layers of cake: red, white, and blue with vanilla icing. Okay, so maybe it did lean, but it was delicious. My dad led us in singing "Happy Birthday". While the custom is for the birthday person to stand quiet and enjoy everyone singing to them, Joaquin joined in with the singing and he was the loudest voice in the chorus. We really had a great time. Joaquin turned the volume on the TV all the way up and he, my dad, and his friends enjoyed watching the game. I remember that night after everyone had left, he turned to me and said, "Thank you." It was more than just the words. It was the look in his eyes. It was a look that said, *"You saw me."* And I did. I saw the little boy in him that just wanted to be loved, seen, and comforted.

I personally believe every wife can see the unseen in her husband, and likewise, the opposite is true for every husband. That's one of the things that I believe causes a man to choose a woman to be his wife. And then the fun begins. Every couple then creates their own dance. They pick their own rhythm, choose their own song, and move through life together in a way that compliments each other. In most cases, that dance is misunderstood by those looking from the outside in. I've come to learn that this is a common occurrence. I've also learned that it is okay.

There were moments in which our dance was misunderstood by others. Maturing as a wife, I learned that it wasn't for others fully to understand, nor was it for us to explain. The function of marriage is intense enough without including the cumbersome work of accommodating the opinions of others.

Juliet Clarke

I was able to see him, and he was able to see me and what we had was a beautiful dance.

Take my parents for example. Once on vacation, I took a photo of my parents sitting poolside doing some reading. My father was reading the autobiography of Sir Winston Churchill and my mother was reading a copy of the National Enquirer. Total opposites. But I always say no one else could stand to be married to my mother but my father and no one else could stand to be married to my father but my mother. They have their own dance and as I type at this moment, their music is still playing forty three years later.

    The dance Joaquin and I chose was one in which he created space for me to have balance and freedom. And he was given space to be seen, heard, valued, and appreciated for the amazing, intellectually gifted, and passionate man that he was. In this world, he was always encouraged to give attention to those areas of himself that needed support. However, he was always celebrated and accepted. He made sure that I had the things that I needed and much of what I wanted. Even though I didn't go through our marriage constantly asking him for things, he just paid close attention to things I did not say. The ability that my husband had to be intuitive to my emotional needs was something that I honestly believe God gave him. In our home, he made sure that the premium was placed on me "being" and not "doing."

CHAPTER 3
"MY MOMMA, WHAT'S UP JAZZ, HI DAD"

"My Momma"

My family always treated *Joaquin* with respect. He was included and he had a place of his own. He created and developed his own relationship with each member of his new family and loved each of them for his own personal reasons.

For my mom, he was a laughing companion and fellow movie buff. I also think they bonded over having similar life experiences of growing up as "city" kids. My mother truly enjoyed having a son. She would often call Joaquin with all her tech issues, and he would happily drop everything, including me, to help install, set up, delete or program anything she needed. He affectionately called her *"Momma"* and their relationship was so beautiful to watch. He spoiled her. Whenever he would make his famous coleslaw, he had to set aside a bowl for her. Joaquin was not phony at all, and I think he was so close to my mom because she provided for him a maternal love that supported him in his areas of challenge, yet still communicated his worth and value as a person via the love she would show him. Never afraid to confront him with love as a mother should, she also never used words that damaged him. My mom has a saying, *"Don't mess with my ducklings,"* speaking of the protective nature she has over my sister and I. I remember the day that Joaquin and my mother were watching television together and she turned to him to let him know that he was now one of her "ducklings." He had the biggest smile on his face. True to his nature, he then turned to me and said, *"Well I guess you're out Ju, 'cause I'm the favorite now!!*

"What's Up Jazz?"

Now my sister was another story altogether. I remember being so afraid to have them meet initially because my sister is also one who doesn't hold her tongue. So, two people firmly committed to speaking frankly in the same space could be a bit scary. The time had finally come for them to meet. It was one Sunday after church. Joaquin was in the Gill Hall of our church and my sister went in to meet him. What they didn't know was that I was standing on the other side of the partition wall barely breathing and waiting to join in if an intervention was needed. After a few moments of introduction and my sister's line of questioning, the conversation took on a lighter tone surrounding the music. From that moment on, they would enjoy many laughs over me and their mutual love of music. My sister appreciated how my husband secured and protected me. While she is the younger, she is the stronger personality. After she got to know him for herself, they began to share a true brother-sister bond. One day she was visiting my house with a friend, and we were enjoying a laugh in the kitchen. My husband called to me from the "cave" asking me to bring him something. Being slightly annoyed at his interruption of our laugh, I called back to him, *"Hold on a minute"*. My sister said to me, *"Oh no, you better stop right now and get him whatever he is asking for because you got a good thing going here and you can't come back home."* Of course, my friend and I laughed even harder at her blunt interpretation of that moment. I reluctantly left the kitchen to attend to whatever it was that he asked for and we continued to enjoy our time together.

"Hey, Dad!!!"

Now, remember I promised you honesty so I must tell you the first few moments between my dad and my husband were a bit bumpy. As it has been established, my husband's personality was larger than life, and anyone who knows my dad knows that he doesn't do well with those who bang the door in. He responds better when you calmly knock and wait to be invited in, the exact opposite of the way my husband preferred to introduce himself.

There was great concern for me about how these two men who were so close to my heart would connect. My father and my husband had to find their own rhythm, so to speak. Once again, I thank God for the wise women he has placed in my life who encouraged me not to get involved but to allow them to work it out amongst themselves. The fixer in me wanted to intervene but I learned that as men, they had to go through their process differently. Me, being my father's daughter, had to be reconciled with me, being my husband's wife. I don't think there is anything that can prepare a woman for that balancing act. The thing that is so hard to express is that one function does not automatically negate the other. Becoming my husband's wife did not instantly make me disengage from being my father's daughter. All my innate "daddy's girl" instincts didn't just leave at the wedding, nor do I think they should've had to. I had to learn how to navigate that path while remaining fully present in both my function as a daughter and wife. I must say I didn't get it right as much as I would've wanted to. Eventually, I found a rhythm for myself in this area that seemed to work for us.

Once they came to their place of agreement, their relationship became something that I enjoyed watching. My father gave my husband the nickname "MD". My husband worked as a nurse administrator, but he always told me that his ultimate childhood dream was to be a doctor. Given a different foundation, he no doubt would have been able to realize that dream. My father giving him that nickname reinforced the view of himself in that area. He would often tell me *"I just want to make dad proud."* I would then retort, *"Well then you're going to have to be quiet."* And we would laugh. I also believe that my dad respected my husband for how he cared for me. It wasn't the material items that were appreciated, it was the fact that my father (by his own words) was not concerned with whether I was secured and protected. I always told my husband that he got extra "manhood" points in this area because his life experiences did not give him a road map as to how to properly be the "head of the home" in function more so than in name. By Joaquin making the choice not to repeat the patterns that caused him damage, it allowed my dad to gain that respect for him. Joaquin would always invite my dad to our home to watch the game with him. Soon after the game, the conversation would turn to music or church experiences of the past. There were many times when I would leave them to enjoy their conversation and I loved that my dad was able to enjoy the experience of having a "son in love".

    Ultimately, my husband was a great addition to my

family. He became the resident doctor, the tech department, and of course someone to share and enjoy a laugh with. We were so happy to have him. My Aunt Jeanie would always call and say, *"How's my nephew?"* She enjoyed laughing with him over holiday meals and his many funny stories. With us, he belonged. He was a part and I know that was a prayer answered for him.

CHAPTER 4
I GOT TO THE GOLD

From time to time, I would struggle with certain aspects of my husband's personality, that is the name of the game in marriage. If you are not willing to deal with challenges, then it's best to remain foot loosed and fancy-free because the requirements for being a girlfriend are much less strenuous than the responsibility of being a wife. It's not for the faint of heart or for the woman looking to marry Jesus' little brother.

My father and I got closer throughout my marriage because there were things about men that only he could help me to understand. He was the one who encouraged me to dig a bit beyond the "what" to the "why". He would always say to me, *"Juliet, a husband is a responsibility and GOD is going to hold you accountable for how you attend to that responsibility."* Then in moments of severe challenge, he would say, *"Juliet, a marriage is not something that you just throw away."* For as long as I can remember, my father said something to me about my husband that I used as my main objective in growing in my role as his wife. One day I was particularly distressed in my spirit over something my husband said on his social media page. I called my dad in a rage, and he let me get all the steam out and then he calmly said to me, ***"Juliet, there is gold buried in Joaquin. You just have to ask God for the tools to mine it out."*** I will be forever grateful to my father for having the wisdom of a sage at that moment. First, because in exasperation my hands were quickly about to find their way around my husband's neck. And, secondly, those words caused me to switch my whole perspective on my husband.

    Unfortunately in life, you don't get to pick your childhood trauma. Subsequently, you don't get to pick how unresolved trauma presents itself in your life. Dr. Nadine Burke Harris, M.D. did some extensive research in this area of development which she describes in her book "The Deepest Well". It is defined as an ACE or Adverse Childhood Experience. This is described as a child being exposed to one or more of the following during their period of development: physical abuse, sexual abuse, emotional abuse, physical neglect, mental illness, divorce, and substance abuse. As an Early Childhood Educator, myself, I know that for a child having a voice that is valued, validated, and heard is vital for proper growth and development. At certain points of a child's development if that child is not nurtured and valued it can cause a child to question whether they are loved or even wanted. This child can grow up to become an adult who searches for acceptance and comfort in a myriad of different things: drugs, alcohol, sex, food, illegal activity, etc. When a child does not feel safe in their home and searches for and requests a home elsewhere, that is a sign that they are not receiving what they need at that point in their development. Living with my husband in what I now realize were his final years here on earth taught me how vitally important the childhood years are to the proper growth and development of an individual.

    Of course, it was easy for me to join the chorus and address the surface presentations of my husband's trauma presented. However, as a wife, I had a responsibility to *find the gold.* It started with me drawing a boundary on what I listened to. I would not allow anyone from my husband's past to fill me with stories of his shortcomings and pitfalls. I also would not allow anyone to pollute me with their opinions of him that focused only on his challenges. Then, I asked God to help me to magnify his strengths, his abilities, and his God-given talents. I always said my husband had the ability to see people. A story was told to me of a nursing school friend of his who was struggling with passing the NCLEX which is one of the two standardized tests nurses need to pass to become a registered nurse. This friend explained to me how she had failed her first attempt and was seriously considering changing her career path. She made the mistake of telling Joaquin her plan to quit. Not only did he not allow her to quit but he committed himself to helping her to pass the tests. She described how he committed several weekends to help her study into the wee hours of the morning. He would share with her his notes and drill her on the material. She credits Joaquin with her being a registered nurse to this day because he refused to let her quit.

That desire to see everyone succeed was some of the gold that I believe my father encouraged me to find. My husband would help anyone find a job. I can't tell you how many times he would help his friends organize and present their resumes. A fierce defender of the underdog, if he felt that someone was being mistreated, he was an opponent you did not want to have to face. There again was some of the gold buried within him.

I believe God gave my husband the ability to draw people. He was the only person I know that maintained friendship relationships in all the areas of his academic life all the way back from elementary school. Seeing and cultivating the value in others, supporting friends through difficult times, bringing a smile to an overcast face, and making a meal for someone in need, were just some of the flecks of gold that made Joaquin the remarkable man that he was.

Reflection causes me to realize that God selected me to provide a space for the best of him to shine. As his wife, it was my responsibility to find that gold and mine it out. I tried to the best of my ability and as much as he would allow me to do just that. As his lady, I used every tool I had to communicate to him his worth and value as a person.

Throughout our marriage, I saw the transformation take place in him. The anxiety of forcing himself to fit for fear of being rejected was replaced with the peace of knowing that his place was secured. Holidays became his favorite time as he would always invite everyone to our home (most times without even telling me how many people he intended for us to feed).

My father was right. There was gold buried in him and I am so grateful to God for giving me the tools to "mine it out".

CHAPTER 5
THE WORST NIGHT OF MY LIFE

For some time, Joaquin had been complaining of pain in his lower abdomen. Everyone knows that nurses and doctors make the worst patients. Truer words have never been spoken. I asked him on several occasions to go and get an exam. Every wife must decide between nagging and peace, which also meant me deciding to stop bugging him about going to the doctor. This is something that I grappled with in the dark hours after he passed away. Should I have just been a nag and annoyed him until he went? Should I have just made the appointment myself and forced him to go to the doctor? If you knew Joaquin, then you knew that there was no such thing as making him do anything he didn't want to do. Once his mind was made up about something there wasn't much room for a changed mind. The lesson for me was that you can do what you can for your loved ones but there is always that space where you must give your loved ones the right to make their own decisions. Through grief therapy, wise counsel, and prayer I was able to realize God doesn't force his will on us. He gives us the right to choose and make our own decisions. My husband was very intelligent, and he was very medically aware; having medical knowledge over and above the average person. In retrospect, I believe that there came a point when he suspected that what he was dealing with was serious and he didn't want to alarm me. He just didn't want to deal with it. That was his choice to make and I have learned that I have to respect that. It wasn't my fault and it didn't mean that I wasn't a capable wife. It was simply his choice and I had to leave it at that.

  On what I have come to call the worst night of my life, we were home and he was just really suffering. With some carefully chosen words, I was able to convince him to go to the ER to get this pain checked out. I will never forget that night for the rest of my natural life. It was a Thursday in November. I was wearing a pink sweater with black pants and my black uggs. As I drove him to the ER, he was giving me instructions as to what to do with the turkey he had stored in my mom's deep freezer. It was time to start prepping for the thanksgiving dinner meal. When we arrived at the hospital, they prescreened him and he was given a room in the ER. One of the nurses was nice enough to give me a chair so that I could stay with him. Then the testing and blood draws began. I remember thinking this is taking an awfully long time even for the ER. Surprisingly, it wasn't very crowded so, I didn't expect to have to wait as long as we did. There is nothing, absolutely nothing that could have prepared me for the next moment when it felt like my life stopped. I was sitting in the chair and my husband was reclined in the hospital bed. The ER Doctor came into the room, closed the door, and pulled a chair up to the bedside. **"Mr. Clarke, according to the x-ray, you have cancer and it has metastasized to your liver and your lower right lung."** My husband and I locked eyes with each other and I vividly remember the color slowly washing away from his face. He looked from the doctor to me and then back to the doctor and then fixed his gaze on the ceiling and sat frozen. As the doctor continued to talk, he snapped back into awareness and began to ask questions. Me, on the other hand, the next few moments were a real blur. Most things I have forgotten, but there are a few things that remain quite clear in my recollection. I remember having to struggle for breath and I remember all of a sudden feeling extremely cold and beginning to shake. I walked to the other side of the hospital and found an empty ladies' room. I locked the door behind me and immediately dialed my mother. As soon as I heard her voice, I broke. I let out a wail that came from a place so deep that digging down to get it out exhausted me. Through a cascade of tears and broken words I was able to get it out, *"He has cancer, Mommy."* My mother being the pillar of strength that she is was able to calm me down and readjust my mind. I had curled my body up into a ball on the bathroom floor and my face was glued to the floor by my tears. I had married my husband just two- and one-half short years before this horrible night. Just the week prior, we were discussing our plans to celebrate our third wedding anniversary. It felt like this had to be some sort of a sick joke. There was no way this could be happening. This was the official beginning of what I came to call the "fog" that I lived through for the next four months of my life.

After my mother had put me back together again, I left the bathroom and returned to the bedside of my husband. At this point, the shock had completely left him and true to his nature he had the ER doctor in stitches laughing about something he had said. When he caught my eyes, he said to me, *"Come here Pook."* I walked over to his bed and took his hand. *"I'm going to be fine and we are going to beat this because I am not going to leave you."* Then he said to me, *"I don't want you to tell anyone because I don't want people to think I am weak."* I agreed with him and assured him that I would keep this confidential. The doctors had determined to admit him to the hospital so that they could complete some further testing and make some determinations regarding the specifics of his diagnosis. I don't know how I made it home that night but somehow despite the ocean of tears that ran down my face, I made it to my driveway. Now here is where again, I will choose to be completely transparent. Being a person of faith, I wish I could tell you that I grabbed a bottle of "blessed oil" and went into serious prayer. Unfortunately, I did not. My initial response was shock. I remember sitting in the Jeep and saying out loud to GOD, *"Are you really allowing this to happen to me?"* I felt so deserted and I felt so alone. No one in my age group or peer circle had ever dealt with anything like this and then for me to honor my husband's request, was further isolation. I couldn't even talk about it. Eventually, *Joaquin* allowed me to share what we were facing with one of my closest friends; Shardae. She had married my childhood friend, Justin, and we had become very close. I will never understand the stress she felt walking with me through every step of this process. By profession; she's also a licensed social worker, so I'm sure in many of my psychotic moments she had to rely on her formal education along with her Holy Ghost. It felt like God let the bottom drop out of my life. I just could not reconcile with this reality. Little did I know I had just been enrolled in a class called "The Sovereignty of God". I learned it was a beautiful thing to sing about, but a horrible thing to experience if it went in a different direction from what your personal petition is.

From this point forward, I buried my head down and did whatever had to be done to make sure my husband had everything he needed to beat this thing. I was absolutely determined that he was going to stand before the church and give his testimony of miraculous healing. I got my hands on every supplement, herb, and vegetable I could find that was studied and proven to have aided in the cure of cancer. I researched every website and went as far as ordering natural herbs from other countries to give him. I made friends with his medical team and forced myself to become acquainted with all the medical terminology so that I could have clear conversations with them regarding his treatment and care. I would wake up, go to work (at the time I was teaching 2nd grade), go home, change clothes, get whatever he needed, and head for the hospital. I would stay until the wee hours of the morning, go home, wash off and do it all over again. The best way to describe this part was a **DARK CLOUD**. There was never a day when uncertainty, confusion, and fear weren't gripping me.

      At the onset of the diagnosis in retrospect, I went

into survival mode. You know that space where you are not really feeling or hearing or being present in your life? You are just getting through Monday, Tuesday, Wednesday, Thursday, and Friday. I had no appetite, and I couldn't sleep at night, or very long. I lost over twenty pounds and it wasn't a good weight loss. At this point I needed reinforcements. I was doing the best I could to hold on, but my grip was becoming unstable. I talked to my husband, and he consented to allow me to share what we were facing with Shardae's mother, Mother Artice Hale. She is a mighty woman of God, with a powerful prayer life.

    I have always been blessed to be surrounded by wise women. Growing up as a young girl, I was always around older women because my parents were working hard to build the ministry. I would love to sit amongst my mom and her first lady friends and quietly take in all that they were saying. I can remember some of my fondest memories were when my mom was in a group called Women's Christian World or WCW under the direction of Dr. Phyllis Carter. My mom, worked along with the late

Rev. Nora Johnson, who she assisted, and I would love to sit and listen to their planning meetings and administrative sessions. Little did I know I was learning the mechanics of running a ministry from the inside out. My mom would have to attend these meetings and I would beg to go with her, rushing to get all my homework done so I could go with her when she was ready to leave. Dr. Carter and my mom would meet at Dr. Carter's office with the group and the meeting would begin. I would always sit in the middle of the couch with my coloring book on my lap. Prayer would open the meeting and then it would begin. I absolutely loved it. My toys and items were packed to keep me occupied always went untouched because I would be very much involved in listening to the meeting. From then until now, I have always had a love for being in the company of wise women who have life experiences. Mother Hale was one of those women. When I shared with her what was going on, her very first response was, *"We are going to pray and you are going to go to war for your husband. I'm going to show you how."* She made for me a prayer plan, complete with scriptures and warfare prayers for me to read and pray at strategic times.

One evening she came over to my home with her sister and they prayed in my husband's man cave. He was upstairs in bed and when they left and I returned upstairs to check on him, he asked me how many women had been praying in the cave. I told him just three and he said it sounded like an army of women were praying. He said when Mother Hale was praying it felt like the house was shaking.

For the next couple of weeks, I followed the prayer plan exactly how she laid it out for me and I can honestly say it got me through and helped to keep me sane in my mind. At this point, I truly believed that God was going to heal my husband on this side of heaven, and this was going to be a great testimony. I even went to the length of telling the doctors, respectfully of course, that they were going to be shocked when they saw that he was going to be healed. I was in a routine of praying and fasting for my husband and I believed beyond a shadow of a doubt that my prayer would be answered in the way that it was requested. Mother Hale showed me that as a wife, I had the authority in the spirit to pray for and over my husband and that could bind and lose things in the natural and in the spiritual realm. She helped me to understand that as a wife, I had the power to speak certain things over my husband that could break strongholds, generational curses, and demonic bloodline assignments. I look back now and realize that these prayers were not so much curative as much as they were defensive.

Being a man's wife is a heavy responsibility. It is so much fun to have a wedding and go on a honeymoon. By all means, enjoy it all. Nothing wrong with that. But once you get back home and unpack your bags, the real work of being a wife and then learning the nuances of being your husband's wife begins. I had to learn quickly that while I had watched my mom do it for years and there were many things that I learned and was able to implement, there were also some things that I had to learn that my husband needed from me. Spiritually speaking, I was being called upon at this moment to pray my husband through. My husband found God on his own. Unlike myself, he wasn't born and raised in the church. While he was away in college long before he met me, he accepted Jesus Christ as his personal Lord and Savior. During a choir rehearsal one night (he always loved to sing), he describes it as the most intense feeling he'd ever felt in his life. He says that while they were rehearsing a worship song he began to cry and he realized that what he was feeling was the presence of God. He had never felt anything like that before. Before this moment, he considered himself agnostic which meant that he did not believe that there was sufficient evidence to prove the existence of God. After that moment in rehearsal, he always knew for himself that God existed. His friend lead him in the prayer of salvation and he began his own personal relationship with God at that point. He knew how to pray, and he knew how to navigate through spiritual things being a member of New Greater Bethel under the leadership of the late Apostle John H. Boyd, Sr. I watched him apply the lessons he learned from his time there to his diagnosis. He would carry a bottle of "oil" that Dr. Boyd had blessed and he kept his prayer cloth close by. He understood the power and the value of prayer for himself.

His time spent as an active member of that church was among some of the happiest moments of his life.

He often recalled a memory to me and my dad about how he had completed bible school there at the church and his father came to his graduation. He would beam and smile when he talked about how happy it made him to see his dad sitting in the audience as he received his religious degree. Through life's challenges and childhood experiences, certain strongholds existed that could only be destroyed through seriously committed prayer and that is where God used me.

I was having a conversation with Mother Hale after everything was over and she said to me, *"Your prayers helped him to transition."* The prayer warrior was birthed in me, and I became extremely concerned with the atmosphere and environment in our home. My father came over and would pray with my husband and they would have a dynamic time of prayer together. At this time, I was very selective about who was allowed in my home. And yes, I had to make some tough decisions, because I understood as his wife that God was working on him. I witnessed first-hand how my husband's countenance began to change. He became much more concerned with the Word and his private prayer time than much of anything else. Yes, blood is thicker than water, but the spirit is thicker than blood and the covenant of marriage is stronger than that. I had taken full authority over the atmosphere in my home, and I was speaking to the atmosphere. What I realize now is that God was working on my husband internally and preparing him while he was negotiating his own life.

Altogether, Joaquin was hospitalized three times. The third and final time was the most trying. While at this point he didn't talk much, there were moments when I would be there with him and he would just ask me to listen. The contents of those moments I will forever hold close to my heart as much of it was his own personal thoughts about certain people, places, events, and circumstances he had dealt with in his life. One thing, in particular, I will never forget is when he looked at me and said, *"Listen Pook, I don't want a quiet cold boring service. I want a hot service with good music, good singing, good preaching and I want y'all to be laughing."* At this point, I was fully committed to seeing the manifestation of my prayers and I was not entertaining anything other than that, so I said to him, *"Okay, Joaquin, if that is what you want, but you won't be going anywhere anytime soon."* That was among the final verbal conversations we had as he had gotten very quiet at this point. He turned his head and went to sleep and I continued to read the healing scriptures out loud while he slept. Then he woke up and I could tell that he was talking out loud to God. He began to say some things and I grabbed my phone to record it because I just wanted to have a record of it. He said repeatedly, *"I know the reason now. I know the reason. The whole purpose is to serve the Lord."* What I realize now is that he was reconciling his life and preparing to make his transition.

TWO DAYS LATER, JOAQUIN WOKE UP IN GLORY.

That moment was horrifying for me but during that space, I will never forget the peaceful look on his face. He had a glow. He was always a handsome man, but at that time his complexion was bright, and he looked so good. The night before, I had shaved his beard and he looked so good. My husband was gone, and like my father once said, ***"There is nothing more final than death"***.

CHAPTER 6
CELEBRATING THE LIFE OF MY YUMMY

> **I was so vested in the belief that God was going to heal my husband and restore him on this side of heaven that it took a while for the reality of what had just happened to really sink in. Honestly, I don't think it really did until everything was over.**

My friend Tera was with me in the room along with my dad when Joaquin transitioned, and I remember the nurses surrounding me and sitting me down. Up until this point, I had been very composed and in control when I had to deal with them. Thank God for my Aunt Raine who would translate all the medical jargon for me and tell me the questions to ask and the things to request so I was never at their mercy. At this moment, I couldn't talk. I heard the words I wanted to say in my head, but when they would come out, they didn't make intelligible sense. I honestly think Tera had to carry me because my legs stopped working. I remember being placed in the passenger seat of her car and having an overwhelming urge to go home. I wanted to be in our home with his things and alone. The Lord will forgive her for her colorful explanation, but I now know that the plan was never for her to bring me home…LOL. I had to call Shardae to let her know he was gone because she had been praying for him when I told her I was going up to the hospital that morning. She picked up the phone and all I could get out was "Shardae" and when she heard my tone she began to say, *"No, no, no, no."* I said, *"He's gone, Sha."* That's all I could get out. When Tera pulled into my mom's driveway, my sister Jasmine came out of the house and literally picked me up and carried me inside. My mother was sitting in the family room, and I fell into her lap just like I was a child and wailed so hard my whole body shook.

All I could hear was my mother's voice through her own tears saying, *"Oh, my God. My baby. God, my baby."*

I think the composure and the deportment I had been using for the last few weeks with all the things I had been dealing with just all came out in my mother's lap. My father had been in the room with me, and I realize now I don't even remember him leaving the hospital with us. But he somehow got back home. When he walked in through my deep sobs, I asked him if he could "call Joaquin's spirit back" and he peacefully looked at me and said, *"No baby, he's not coming back."* The next few hours were really a blur. I don't think I bathed or ate for almost three days straight. I was at my mom's house, and I was only allowed to use my phone at certain times. Then my mom or my sister would take it. The only time I could think straight was when I was actively planning his homegoing celebration. I took that very seriously as it was the last thing I could do as **Mrs. Joaquin Clarke** to honor him. Often people would speak of him through the lens of his shortcomings and from the perspective of the pitfalls that he suffered in life. My determination as his wife was to ensure that his celebration was first, exactly what he wanted, and secondly, reflective of the intelligent, wonderful man that he was. As his wife, that was solely my responsibility. And with the help of God, my family, and friends I was able to do just that. So, the planning had to begin.

Joaquin's celebration of life was held on a Saturday in March and when the day arrived, I still had trouble wrapping my head around it. At this point and time, my house was filled with friends and family. I was never alone. I woke up that morning and went to get some things I needed from the store. My childhood friend Syreeta was over one night helping me to put the obituary together. Being an educator herself, she helped me to make sure everything was grammatically correct. I will always remember her coming over one day and forcing me out of bed. I still don't know how she got into the house. I just remember her pulling the covers back and saying, *"You need to get out of bed Juliet."* When I tried to whine and beg her to let me stay in bed, true to her nature, she interrupted me and forced me out of bed and downstairs. My close friend Katrina had been staying with me. She had come up from Florida and I remember rattling off to her all the plans I made for that morning. In her very calm Katrina way, she let me know that I wouldn't have time to do all the things I wanted to do and since she was with me, we were going to arrive at my church on time for Joaquin's celebration. Katrina has been in my life since I was around 17 years old, and she has always been the friend who can give a strong dose of reality with a good amount of humor mixed in, so the medicine goes down smoothly. After the dust settled, she admitted to me that she had no intention of letting me do all the things that I planned to do that morning. After Katrina helped me to get dressed, we got in the car, and she drove me to the homegoing celebration for my husband. It felt like the longest ride of my life, but Katrina got me there on time, as was her goal.

From the prayer to the benediction, it was a hot service just like Joaquin wanted. I had poured over every detail to ensure that things were exactly the way I wanted them to be in honor of my husband. I asked Elder Robin Alford, to give the prayer of comfort at the beginning of the service. She and I have always shared a special relationship and she was one of the few who made Joaquin feel comfortable and accepted in my world. She has a special anointing to pray and to pray in difficult situations. When she took the microphone and began to pray the entire atmosphere shifted and it felt like a revival. *She strapped the whole church on her back and climbed us up into the presence of God and took authority over everything that thought it was going to frustrate the service.* Her prayer set the tone for that service, and I will always be grateful to her for allowing God to use her at that moment. I needed her prayers. My friends had been calling me and telling me that they were coming to sing, play instruments and do whatever else I needed them to do. Joaquin had made his impression on them with his dynamic personality and so they wanted to help me celebrate him.

    I remember I was on the phone with Pastor James Lamb. He and his wife, Adrienne, are good friends of mine. Even before the celebration Adrienne had bought over bundles of food for my house and made sure that my kitchen was well stocked. I will never forget them for that. When my father realized that I was on the phone with

Pastor James, or JD, as we call him, my dad said, *"Tell Pastor Lamb I said sing until the yoke breaks."* When I told JD that, he said, *"Yes sir,"* and I must tell you that is exactly what he did. Remember my husband was a singer and he wanted to have good music. So, my dad suggested that we have praise and worship. Pastor Lamb is anointed to usher in the presence of God and that is exactly what he did.

Growing up in church, all the "church kids" form a cohort because we all are growing up together. Pastor Justin Cunningham and I, along with Min. Keibway Greaves grew up in church together. As adults, we are all actively involved in ministry. I asked Pastor Cunningham to be the musical director for the homegoing service and put all the music together with the help of my friends. Min. Greaves, Elder Byron Preston Jr., Prof. Eugene Reid, and the band was AMAZING!! I remember watching them play and thinking how much Joaquin would have enjoyed listening and singing along. I can't even begin to tell you about the singing. You know it's funny. I realized during this process that all my close friends can sing, and I mean sing for real. Like sing until the hair stands up on the back of your head. It kind of makes me scratch my head a bit. Clearly, the singing gene skipped over me. When I looked over to the left of the sanctuary and saw the village of people who came from far and near to sing in the ***Joaquin Clarke Memorial Choir*** that day, my heart was so full. Many of these singers were those who had professionally recorded their own music and they was singing in the choir at my husband's homegoing. I will be forever grateful to them for their contribution and their time. The choir sang two songs: one was led by Elder Jeffery Roberson, and the other was led by Shardae. Both sang with such passion that it felt like the church was literally going to lift off the floor. My husband was so loved by all his friends from far and near and many people wanted to come and show support for me and my family that it became clear that there was going to be a lot of people at this service. Usually, I handle the logistics when we have large services at my church. That's just one of the things that the "PKs" do. In my mind, I was going to do the same thing again because I wanted to make sure things went the right way. Well, my friends know me very well and they know the ridiculousness of my mind. Lady Alexis Preston and Elder Ashley Crandle, close friends of mine, handled all the logistics for me that day and made sure that every Bishop, Pastor, Elder, Minister, and Elect Lady was properly seated and attended to. I'm sure there were things going on behind the scenes, but they are such professionals that they never let on. I can hear Lady Alexis in my head saying, *"You're going to sit down and be Mrs. Clarke and Ashley and I will handle everything else"*. I will never forget them for their sacrifice of time and talent to help that day go so smoothly. Right before my dad gave the eulogy, I asked my close friend and fellow "PK" sister, Pastor Melaine Rochford, to sing the sermonic selection for me. I always say I want to be like Melaine when I grow up. She makes this "PK" thing look so easy, while for me, I go kicking and screaming sometimes. She just peacefully goes about her way and does it with such grace and dignity. That day she sang my father's favorite song, "I Will Make the Darkness Light". What an amazing job she did. My father did an amazing job eulogizing Joaquin. I was concerned for a moment being that he was going through his own grief. But in the end, being the accomplished preacher that he is, he did what no other one could do, and my dad knows how much I love and appreciate him.

I struggled with whether to speak at the service. My biggest concern was if I would be able to stand and speak. I had attended several homegoing services and in most of them when there was a widow, I took note of the fact that the wife usually did not speak. I was having a conversation with Shardae about it and she said to me, *"You are his wife, and you are the only one that can give perspective on who your husband was Juliet."* I thought about it and realized that she was right. Of all the women in the world, this awesome man had selected me to be his wife and there was no other woman or person that knew him the way I did, and for that, I had to speak for him. My sister Jasmine and my best friend of over 30 plus years, Pastor Alana Blackwell-Hendon, stood on each side of me as I spoke about who Joaquin was, the dignity with which he cared for me, and the void that his absence created in my heart. I was so grateful to GOD for helping me to get through that difficult moment.

After the celebration, the culinary team of my church, under the direction of Sis. Andrea Williams prepared a feast. The food was so good. Everything was prepared with such care and my friends are still talking about how delicious the food tasted. Sis. Andrea is someone who will help everyone, and I will always be grateful to her for the sacrifice of her time and energy to make sure that my friends and family had something good to eat.

The Gill Hall was decorated so beautifully. Mrs. Gayle Cunningham (Pastor Justin Cunningham's mother) took the time to make personalized centerpieces for each table. I still don't know how she did it, but she used different photos of Joaquin and I and created football-themed centerpieces. I appreciated it and I know Joaquin would have LOVED to see all that Giants blue. I will always be grateful to Mrs. Cunningham for taking her time to make those centerpieces for me. I felt so special.

The room décor was elegantly sports-themed. My friend Crystal flew in from Florida to stage the room for me. Again, usually, this is something I do for everyone else, and it is very hard for me not to. Crystal came in and with her mother, Elder Deborah Ross, they made that room look so beautiful. She took the time to attend to every detail and when I walked into the space, I could feel the love that she had for Joaquin and I. It was a sports-themed décor, but it was very elegant. I remember a friend of mine commenting that she wanted to take a picture before everyone sat down to eat. Crystal will never know how much I appreciated her for leaving her life and coming here to do that for me.

Of course, it wouldn't be a celebration for Joaquin if it didn't go out with a bang and when we were done, we were greeted by a slight snowfall at the end of the evening. But thank GOD, everyone made it home safely. After the last guest had left and the final condolence card had been given, it was all over. I remember wanting to greet everyone who had come to celebrate him and support me. After the service had ended, I got up to take a sip of water and before I knew it, all I could see was people everywhere, everyone hugging, praying, and giving me their words of support. I was so grateful to have all this love, but I will admit I felt overwhelmed. It felt like out of nowhere Dr. Regina Williams grabbed my hand. She is a fellow "PK" herself and now Bishop's wife, married to his grace, Bishop Fabian Williams. My mother went into labor with me in her mother's car so that's how long our families have been close. She took my hand and I remember that tight grip she held my hand with and somehow, she was able to get me from the sanctuary into the office. I will always be grateful for her at that moment. I affectionately call her "Auntie Co-Pastor" because of what her family has meant to my family. Her mother, Mother Eva Woodside, stood as my grandmother at our wedding and two of her other daughters (who are also like my aunties) were there that day singing in the choir. Elder Charmise Desire' and Sis. Tabreeca Woodside (who was my parents' flower girl at their wedding over forty years ago). The Woodside family will never know how much it meant to me to see them there.

  The floor had been vacuumed, the food had been cleaned up, the lights had been turned off, and the church

Juliet Clarke

doors locked. It was over. It was finished.

*__I had done the last thing
I could do for my husband.
I had fulfilled my final responsibility
as his wife and now it was time
for me to face this reality.__*

CHAPTER 7
DARK

Darkness is the absence of color, light, or sunshine, having a gloomy or evil overcast. That one word characterized my life for the following days and months. It felt like I had been taken to the top of a cliff and pushed off without a parachute. Free falling from the sky, barreling quickly towards the ground. I had stopped eating completely and rarely took off my pajamas and bathrobe. I had never in my life dealt with such a low level of despair. I couldn't see anything in front of me. Everything was dark. I never opened my shades or turned-on lights. I would sit in the dark for hours. Sleep was something that never came. I think my body was so used to staying alert for phone calls from the hospital that I never really relaxed. I know my family wanted me back home, but I didn't want to leave my house. I wanted to be with his things and in the space, we shared as man and wife. I slept in his pajamas at night and wore his shirts and shorts throughout the day. My husband was a big guy, so, me wearing his clothes for several days on end without bathing or changing was not a good sight. My sister Jasmine became a staple in my house. She would frequently come in, clean, and force me to shower and make sure that I ate something. I would chew for a few minutes, but I couldn't keep any food down. I remember the night that devastation gripped me so hard. I couldn't breathe. I couldn't think and I had decided at that moment that I didn't want to live anymore. I wanted to go and be with my husband. I felt so disjointed without him. It's not a cliché, or a fairy tale, the two really do become one flesh and the part of me that went with him was stronger than the part of me that was left here.

I kept replaying conversations with doctors, with myself, and with the Lord. I kept going over and over every detail. I needed something to logically make sense, and nothing was giving me that satisfaction. I felt such a heavy sense of loss and defeat. In those early moments, I carried such a burden of guilt and shame. You know you read the bible for years and years and you never really focus on certain things until life changes your perspective. I realized during this time that the shame of the widow that the bible talks about is real. I felt shame and embarrassment. I couldn't stand being around people. I felt shame for my church family. I felt that in some way I had inflicted such pain on them. They all had accepted Joaquin and he had built his own relationships with them. And now with him being gone, I had somehow caused their grief and pain. I couldn't pray because at that moment I felt like God had left me, He wasn't hearing me, or He was angry with me. In my mentality and emotions, I was spiraling down fast.

I remember the night I decided that I couldn't take it anymore and that I was going to take my own life. I knew this was wrong, but I didn't think I had any other option for peace. The devil took full advantage of my self-imposed distance from God. I had willingly disconnected from my personal power source and my spirit was no longer able to fight off the attacks. That suicide demon would sit on the edge of my bed and talk to me, and I would listen. Thoughts like, *"Why are you staying here? To teach 2nd grade? You're going to hurt like this for the rest of your life. God doesn't love you. Why else would* *he allow you to hurt like this?"* These and many more thoughts filled my head, and I could no longer reason correctly. It wasn't until I experienced this level of grief and depression that I understood that there are such low levels of emotional pain that are unsustainable. I had already decided to take my own life. I just hadn't figured out exactly how to do it. I still had to figure out the plan. I had spoken to Shardae and asked her to handle making sure that everyone got the personal items I wanted them to have, and that my Mom got the note I was planning to leave. In retrospect, she never fully agreed but she definitely supported me in that very low and dark moment of my life. In the meanwhile, I used alcohol to numb the pain. My husband hated alcohol and it wasn't until then that I kept it in the house. I would have to drink to calm my nerves. I still couldn't sleep, but at least I could stop the racing thoughts going through my head. I had written out my plans and decided who I wanted to have my personal belongings and who would carry out my final wishes. It wasn't so much that I wanted to die, as much as living had just become intolerably painful. This is something that I have heard all my life, but I never experienced it on this level until I had gone through this. The prayers of the righteous really do avail much. I KNOW I had an army of people near and far praying for me. Those prayers refused to let me go.

There were times I could feel the tug of war in the spirit realm over me. I had come into agreement with darkness because I wasn't strong enough to fight it off, but the devil never banked on the army of those people praying until those chains broke off my mind and my spirit. They prayed until there was a crack in the darkness, and I was able to see glimmers of light. They prayed until I stopped "sipping" and started speaking the word over my own self. I remember one day Pastor Lisa Jackson was visiting with me. She would come by with the most delicious food. I'm convinced she had to have prayed over that food because even during the time that I wouldn't eat I would always finish that plate of food that she brought. She's like an atom bomb in the spirit (also a fellow "PK" ☺). One day she had been visiting me and we were talking and started laughing with each other. In my own way, I called myself "saying goodbye to her". She heard what I wasn't saying and looked at me in my face and said, *"I heard you Juliet, but I want you to know it's not going to go the way you think it's going to go."* At that moment the strength and authority in her voice let me know that even though I was not strong enough to fight she was standing in the gap for me along with countless others. And as I type these words today, I realize that…

THE PRAYERS OF THE RIGHTEOUS PRAYED ME BACK TO LIFE.

Along with the prayers, I must also credit my Goddaughter, Harmony Gayle, Shardae, and Justin's newest addition to their family. Around this time, she was about five months old and from time to time I would keep her overnight. It's funny that as turbulent as things were in my life at that time, this little baby girl brought such peace into my home and my life. I have always been very sensitive to the atmospheres that children, especially babies, are in. So, when I knew she would be staying, the night before she got there I would open the windows, play worship music, and set a tone for her to be in my home. When she would wake up and need her bottle I would change her, feed her, and rock her back to sleep. During these times she would not let me put her back down, but she would only sleep if I laid her on my chest. Somehow this little baby would always manage to position her body so that her head was right over my heart, and she would sleep so peacefully. As she slept, I would play worship music and pray, (the only time I could pray during this time is when she was in my home) and the tears would gently fall down my face. The anger, resentment, and disorientation I felt would just melt away in the presence of God. It's like her little spirit was ministering to mine and letting me know that it was time to reconnect to my power source so that the inner healing I needed could really begin. *Princess Harmony* will always have a special place in my heart.

At this point, I had intentionally decided that I was going to allow the Lord to heal me. This is when I learned that there are levels to healing and the first step is being

Juliet Clarke

intentional about wanting it. I didn't think that I could ever be what I used to be, but I knew that I couldn't stand living in the dark the way that I was.

CHAPTER 8
LIGHT

Joaquin and I had been planning to conceive a baby at the time of his diagnosis. So being the planner that I was, I had begun collecting different items to help us prepare for a baby. One of the things was a changing table which I kept stored in our spare room. One day I was laying on the bed having such a bad moment and my eye caught the changing table. I instantly got angry and grabbed a hammer. I smashed that table until this well-put-together piece of artistry was a pile of rubbish on the floor. I refused to clean it up as I felt that the pile was indicative of how I felt on the inside. Remember, my younger sister was in and out of my home checking on me. When she walked past the mess on the floor she said, *"What happened here?"* When my mom saw a picture of it, she said, *"Um, I think you may want to go to grief counseling."* I know in some cases the saints don't like to consider professional counseling as an option. I came across a post on social media that said, **Deliverance deals with the**

demons. Therapy deals with the damage. – Author Unknown. Truer words have never been spoken. I was damaged in my spirit, damaged in my relationship with myself, and my relationship with God was damaged. I needed help. Thank God for the wisdom of my mother to know that I needed this at this time in my life.

Dr. Cheryl Mchunguzi was my grief therapist. She did an amazing job of helping me to navigate through this unknown territory of widowhood and grief and rebuilding my life. She gave me the tools that I needed to have the proper perspective on my experience and reshape how I was processing what was happening. Oh, and did I mention she is a believer also? God surrounded me with an amazing village. Then there was Elder Dakota Kimble. She had been widowed some years before me and she was a family friend. She would always pick up the phone when I would call. She never made me feel like I was a burden to her, and she never told me how crazy I sounded during some of our conversations…LOL. Her spirit was so welcoming and peaceful that even in our phone calls I could feel my spirit regaining strength.

I am also grateful for my mom's best friend, Pastor Theresa Martin. I affectionately call her "Foxy" because she's always been such a boss. One day we were talking on the phone, and she very calmly said to me, *"As you walk along this journey and process your healing, the Holy Spirit is going to reveal to you what happened"*. I was so grateful to her for saying that to me because that's what I needed. I needed God to explain to me what happened. I had married this man and like every wife, I expected that we would do life together. I could have never in my wildest dreams imagined that I would be separated from my husband by death. The expectation is that no one lives forever, but I certainly could not have anticipated his years ending when they did. There were certain turning points in my process of healing that earmarked the journey of my process from darkness to light. I had stopped going to my church. Being a "PK", most of my life events were lived out in living color in front of everyone. This was something that I wanted and needed to work through on my own. I let my parents know that I needed some time, and I didn't know how long it was going to be. I knew this was going to be a slight challenge because of the many roles and responsibilities I carried at my church. But thankfully, my parents allowed me this space, and everything worked itself out.

One Sunday I went to church with Shardae and her father Bishop Harrison Hale was preaching on the woman with the issue of blood. Now, this is a very familiar bible story. One in which I had preached myself and taught in Sunday School and so I was very much aware of the narrative. I had never heard the story of the woman with the issue of blood presented in that manner. He talked about the decision this woman made to find Jesus and actively pursue her healing. I appreciated this message so much because it helped me to come to a place of resolution where I was not going to grapple with this darkness any longer. I was going to intentionally pursue my healing. That day when the altar was opened for prayer, at the leading of the Holy Spirit I went up. When he ministered to me, he said to me "GOD said this is a turning point for you" and GOD's words spoken through him were exactly correct. That was the beginning of the end of the darkness.

I had begun journaling again and listening to worship music in the morning during my personal meditation.

One morning during my time with God, I was quietly listening in His presence, and just like Pastor Theresa told me, the Lord began to explain to me what happened. I struggled very much with thinking that GOD had stopped listening to my prayers or maybe that in some way I wasn't effective in prayer. My Husband was gone, my immediate prospects at being a mother had gone with him and this all made me feel like GOD did not hear my prayers. The Lord said to me, *"I was listening to you, but I was talking to you about what you were saying to me. I wasn't obligated to share with you my conversations with your husband."* While this statement can seem a bit harsh or dismissive, I appreciated God so much for giving me that perspective. I had to realize that he was Joaquin's God too and he had an obligation to grant his petition. This was a turning point because it lifted the burden of uncertainty off me. From this point forward, I began to unpack my pain in the privacy of my prayer closet and let God conduct the difficult surgery of extracting the infection of the lies of

Satan out of the marrow of the bone of my spirit.

During Joaquin's celebration, Archbishop Robert Rochford, a world-renowned first-class Preacher made a statement that helped to categorize this aspect of my healing. He said, *"God will never take someone you love from you without giving you more of himself."* It was painful and ugly and downright horrible at many times, but I can say that these words have become a reality in my life. God did give me more of himself. He took out the pain and filled up the voids with his peace, his love, and his spirit. Even when I had to deal with retaliations from the devil for his anger over the fact that he was defeated and his plan over my husband's life was destroyed, I was able to respond with the love of Christ.

The prayer time I have with God is so intense and passionate, that I can say that he has revealed himself to me in a way that allowed me to meet him in a way that I had not before. God is real and his plan and purpose over my life "WILL" be fulfilled.

My closest friend in the world, Pastor Alana Blackwell-Hendon said words at Joaquin's celebration.

She is a singer and preacher in her own right, and she commanded me to live. She talked about the work that was still left for me to do. You see, Joaquin had fulfilled the ultimate purpose of every believer despite what he had to face in life. He didn't allow that to keep him from finding God and developing a personal relationship with him. He was passionate, he was talented, and he was mine.

CHAPTER 9
WHAT I LEARNED

I can look back now and honestly say that I am grateful for what I learned about God going through this experience.

I never thought I would be able to say that. I never thought I would remain in the land of the living. I learned that there are levels of pain that don't have words. Even in those moments, GOD is still very much near to the brokenhearted. Experiencing the death of my husband and walking through the process of grief, taught me so much about life. Watching Joaquin overcome the things he did, taught me the real value of family. Take the time to love the ones God has given you. When the casket closes, it's too late to say the things you wish you had said and unsay the things that in moments of anger you may have said. Grief is already such a heavy burden but grieving with guilt is despair that can be avoided. Families will disagree and have conflict. This is the business of life. But don't use your words as weapons against your children, your siblings, or loved ones. Those words will live on long after they are gone. Don't say anything that you can't live with, without them. Children should always be made to feel safe, protected, loved, and appreciated. Of course, there is no perfection anywhere. We won't achieve that until we get to glory. However, an honest effort can be made to build and maintain connections with those whom we share genetics with.

The absence of my husband's physical presence in my life has left a void that I can't even begin to describe. As much as I miss him and want him back here for my enjoyment, I am so happy that he is finally free. He is in a place where evil words will no longer haunt him, and evil deeds will no longer hurt his heart. He is free and with his Savior, out of pain, out of suffering, and able to enjoy the pleasures of the paradise of God. After living through the trauma and pain that categorized his life, an early admittance into glory is the only way out that could make his pain worth it. I am so happy he is finally free. In my imagination, I say he has a body that matches his personality and I'm sure he is the loudest voice in the heavenly choir. I am also happy that he left here knowing that I loved him, that I saw him, that I appreciated him and that for me, he was the best husband in the world.

"Continue to enjoy heaven Yummy. You deserve it"!!

KNOW THAT YOU ARE NOT ALONE...
SOMEONE CARES 24/7

National Suicide Prevention Lifeline
Free & Confidential Support
(800)273-8255
OR
Military & Veterans
988

Share Your Experience with the Author

Juliet Clarke
Email: mrsclarke689@gmail.com

Indicate in Subject Line: Tears

Mailing Address
PO Box 982
Manorville, NY 11949

For Booking Requests

Contact
Elaine Jackson
(631)926-7495

www.ingramcontent.com/pod-product-compliance
Lightning Source LLC
Chambersburg PA
CBHW070513090426
42735CB00012B/2765